A Verse for Liberty

A Verse for Liberty:
Poetic Collections

Author & Poet,
Chelsea Jones

XULON PRESS

Xulon Press
2301 Lucien Way #415
Maitland, FL 32751
407.339.4217
www.xulonpress.com

Printed in the United States of America.

Paperback ISBN-13: 978-1-63221-818-6
eBook ISBN-13: 978-1-6322-1819-3

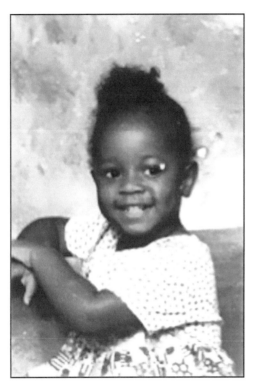

Picture Day at Precious Pals Circa 1997

Dedication:

To my Mother (Ranessa Jones) and Father (Clance Jordan)
To my village -- Hannibal Square, Winter Park, Florida
To souls this is meant to touch

TABLE OF CONTENTS

I Know Who I Am

Hermann Park, 2017

CONFIDENT
2011

I move like the tide of a furious wave

I'm slick like the clean bald head with a fresh shave

I'm deep like the heart of the earth and I'm priceless

Not even the sound of Donald's trump can out play me I move swiftly but gently like "h" in shh I'm alliteratively high off the speed of life making my moves right

Then I stop to look left, but keep going because my right is within myself, unmistakable

I rock the jewels of this land with the essence of happiness in my hand and confidence in my Stand, I am immovable

I don't even show signs of nervousness cause that's tacky and I'm unshakeable

I keep a smile when you see me so you will never will know, unbreakable

My smile shines through adversities and my words tend to cut deep

And my eyes glow brighter than a thousand of Mar's suns

My faith wins fights even when the battle has just begun

I run faster than the Euphrates can flow and I stand taller than any tree can grow

I know more about science than Galileo

Cause I am the definition of any star that floats around Pluto. It's true though

I'm a fiery ball traveling at the speed of 500 kilometers per second cause I'm the, I'm the best - I'm the, I'm the best. And ain't no second guessing

And I don't have to toot my own horn

Because it's obvious that on February 22, 1994 greatness was born

I swarm around all my haters and enemies cause through my accomplishments I sting 'em up like bumble bees then use their negativity for hair treatment as I comb my head with honey Sometimes I think back and it's funny

This time last year I was lower than the structure of any valley

I felt worse than a workout at Bally

And I was more depressed than a stressed single mother

But today I stand with surety. Detecting in my future no obscurity

And it's evident that my confidence is not mistaken for cockiness

I am confident

WOMAN OF COLOR
2012

My name is **Liza** and they ripped the lungs right outta my chest
Beat me till even blood got tired of bleeding they beat me till whip marks made quilted patterns and echoes came from lashes
then he rubbed salt into my back
Can you feel it? Massa caught me reading
He says "you-on need-a read about God, just believe em"
Well I wanted to know for myself. And he caught me in Exodus
I's felt sumn' heavy in the room and I looked up and that was him
Ripped the lungs right outta my chest and I was tryna remember how to breathe like when I had Jesse. I reckon I was partly
surprised cuz I was sure he wasn't gone catch me
And lord all I could think of was how to breathe
Ole Lincoln signed the papers dat says I can be free
But ole Massa won't let me leave
Say I gotta keep on having' his babies like Jesse, Liz, Charles, and Ray

My name is **Rachel** and freedom never had so many chains
Who would have thought wanting a drink of water would result in a matter over race?
Just in case you didn't notice, I have eyes. You have eyes. I have a hand
You have hands so why am I being stripped of the right to function as a human?
Assuming I am not intellectually esteemed, focusing beams on my failures, exploiting my people
I go down into prayer begging God for the chance to experience true freedom
Fighting double the double standards
I must cook, clean, and submit to my husband while still minding my lady manners
While still fighting over matters of black and white black or white
Baby would you like that tie loose or tight, but not too loud
Ladies are supposed to be quiet. Not quite...

Nowadays **we** seem to be winning the fight
Obliterating statistics, living above notions of unrealistic projections
We are conquering emotional, physical, and mental abuse and healing through lessons
We spread our blessings and empower other women of virtue
Building our strength, we possess as women to be unbreakable, powerful, immoveable
It is written that today moving forward we will seek to form prints in sand not known to man
For we are more than our child bearing hips, mother breeding breast, and brother welcoming figure. We are women that have been long time contributing factors and contenders
We have helped to define all of Americas known glories. From Hattie McDaniel to Harriett Tubman are just a few stories of women breaking racial barriers – setting precedence in a world that just seemed to grow all the scarier. These are the mothers from where we draw valor, wisdom and might. Women of all backgrounds can contribute to this beautiful sight
There were thousands of Liza's and ten thousand of Rachel's
Not everyone has to be an Oprah, Maya or Rosa
You can be a Sheryl, Carrol, or Erica
I am Chelsea and I am a black woman contributing to the history and culture of America

We Will Replace Time
2019

I've made up my mind
Time has ceased to exist as a measure of limits
And going forth every choice is mine
We replace time with decisions. No longer will time be used as a means to compare
We replace time with visions
Moments, now, will step outside the box of dates and reign in eternity
We will not settle for expirations
But, rather inspirations where time is replaced with creativity
We replace time with forgiveness
We will not leave it up to years to do the work of healing
Our children will witness
That there is beauty in the work, not in how long the work is done
The race is not given to the swift, but the one who will run
We replace the markings of beginnings and endings with 'You Are Here'
This helps to dispel fear. This helps to draw beauty near
We replace time with lessons
With essence, we will replace time

FOR PAIN & GLORY

Linda's House, 2017

WHAT GOES ON IN THIS HOUSE
2012

Shh You know the rule

What goes on in this house, stays in this house

"And I dare it to get back to me if anybody ever finds out"

It's murder, suffocating the voice of every child that needed to let it go. I nod my head in agreeance. But on the inside, I'm grieving. Dying because of lack of speaking. I can't tell Grandma what happened to me last weekend

If I did it would weaken momma to the core but she's no excuse cause just the other day she called me a whore when the week before I was the one who caught her in the bed with the man from next door. I abhor

The words that come out of her mouth but the rules go as follows

What goes on in this house stays in this house

But in this house the walls are speaking, it tells a story of my sister weeping and it paints a picture with her red blood that daddy beat off the flesh of her body

But shh you can't say a mumbling word. I guess I kind of just have to cope with the hurt so I pick up the phone and I dial his number. It is with him when I am no longer concerned about

What goes on in that house

I sneak out and listen to the words daddy never told me. "You're beautiful, magnificent and there's no need for you to feel lonely" (kiss) he kisses me on the cheek and tries to do that thing that I don't like done to me

I can't because all I could see was his face. "NO!" he wraps his arms around me with embrace and I push him away, me no longer wanting to stay, but I never told him why

It's like he could tell what I wanted to say through my cry. But I was quiet as a mouse, remembering the golden rule, what goes on in this house stays in this house

So, I won't let him love me. I go home only to enter the same mess. I have to confess if I want to be free from the demons that tamper with my mind telling me life isn't worth my time But the Devil is a lie

I figured out that it is within my pen and paper I confide and confess. So, I guess the rule that says what goes on in this house stays in this house, works out for my best

That Girl
2010

It never used to bother me when I'd listen to songs that did not bring Him glory

Surely, I'd bob my head to beats and lyrics that degraded me instead of persuading me of my true worth. Curse words rolled off the tip of my tongue like hamster spin wills and I made deals with the enemy knowing he couldn't save the soul that was within me

My worst enemy was my inner me

I was that girl

I never had a body of a goddess or

Breasts like theatrical puppets, a bottom with consumption of male focal attention or curves with a third-dimension figure

I had figured bulky thighs could never attract male bulging eyes and they'd be alarmed if I had ever tried to charm with chunks for arms

I was that girl

Secretly I had a dire need for this emptiness to be filled, brokenness to be mended a heart that needed to be healed. Secretly I was thirsty, hungry, and searching for safety

I transformed into a walking testimony becoming That Girl

My music became selective, my speech became impressive, my body became corrective to the mind that was within it knowing that I was created in the beauty of His image

I could hear him saying "I wanna use That Girl"

I responded to the call giving up the pleasures of this world

My emptiness was filled with his spirit, my brokenness was mended my heart became his canvas and I became his witness.

God I respect your appointed anointing that you have trusted me with and I seek to be eternally your daughter. I don't mind being that girl

LIKE NOAH
2012

I want the obedience of Noah and Mary's yes
I want faith like David and the blessing of Abraham
Like confidence in Jabez request to enlarge my territory, God I want increase so I decree that You o lord bless me indeed
I wanna be nomadic like Paul spreading good news in streets and in cathedral halls
I want the loyalty of Job and I know I don't have an issue of blood
But can I please touch your robe?
And maybe then I might be healed from self-destruction, self-infliction, man-made addictions this unrighteous condition.
The enemy's hidden mission is to use pure intentions for perverted tactics. Deceiving messages stating I lack this confidence.
But how abundant are bold words and sharp swords waging war against the enemy of my soul
I feel like Matthew. Choosing to drop my pen and stop collecting on men and taxing their sin
Present riches and Christ and I'll take my chances with Christ
Where eternally I will be rich in love, passion, and forgiveness
Bear witness to obedience like Noah

I Woke Up Blessed
2020

It is a beautiful feeling waking up like this
Waking up in such bliss
In truth of who I am and whose I am
Living the kind of life that naturally invokes a high
Instead of the kind of life that unnaturally makes you cry
Trains making glorious sounds and joy being flamboyantly found in the
Hallelujah of birds singing, praising, ringing
I woke up satisfied with the life I'd voice activated
Satisfied with the realities I'd confidently stated
I woke up blessed
I rose up from the bed of peace with all things former released
I woke up with room in my belly
I woke up with a womb of prophetic declarations and beautiful anticipation of today's abundant life that needs nothing
except my permission and participation
I had not even opened my eyes or lifted my chin to the sky when I woke up blessed
I simply felt God massage my chest and I immediately began to meditate on this goodness
This blessing overwhelmed me overtook me overpowered me
For this blessing was bestowed upon me undeservingly, but I have been deemed worthy of this kind of kindness
It's a beautiful feeling waking up like this
I woke up blessed

MR. BIRD
2020

A bird made a nest right outside my window to keep me company

Right outside my window a bird made a nest to keep me from being lonely

A bird made a nest right outside my window to serenade me each morning with its melodies

Right outside my window a bird made a nest so we could have devotion and join in sweet fellowship together

A bird made a nest right outside my window to make me a spectator of his skillful art

Right outside my window a bird found me worthy

A bird made a nest right outside my window to show his trust in me

Right outside my window a bird thanked me for the energy of gratitude and compassion he could feel from the inside of my house

But Mr. Bird, why this tree? Why right in front of me? I remember when this tree had no leaves in its brutal winter peak and both of us used the window as our mirror

A bird made a nest right outside of my window to remind me of glory

To remind me of worth

To remind me of charity

Thank you, Mr. Bird, for building your home right in front of mine

The Rainbow
2012

It never disappeared

Just hid in the shadows and was smeared across a mirror to show a distorted reflection

Old ideologies presently rejected because we haven't seen outburst like this since Lyndon B was president. How relevant are the matters of race so resident in my own back yard

How far have we actually come?

I mean we've overcome parts of physical slavery

We have fought for rights, but attached to that I still have to add maybe

Because sadly lives have succumbed to mentalities that should have died with physical slavery

There are still innocent puddles of blood guilty to only the color of their skin

He was only 17

Tears still bleed his dried blood and hearts are reminded that there is still a ways to go

This is a case that explicitly shows ignorance at its best and a simple arrest could help bring Trayvon rest. But I guess our system is not above defending ignorance

There is justice that must be shown and facts that must be known

No more innocent gravestones

Still it's like a scratch I can't satisfy an alibi I simply cannot justify

How can a pack of a taste the rainbow snack pose as threat of an attack?

Can you taste the many different colors of the rainbow that could possibly symbol the very content of diversity or the lack thereof in a society?

TITLE
2011

And so, it seems, we have become blind and deaf to the power of our existence

Not realizing that the scope of our being is omniscient

We have lost sight of ourselves as we both consciously and unconsciously rebel against the natural intellect that has crowned us queens and kings

But to the facts we are obscene and we no longer believe that we are of royal status

The few aspirations we've set for ourselves are basketball players dope pushers and rappers

What are we doing?

What is the goal in mind that we should be pursing?

Claiming to be a part of the game not realizing that in actuality we're losing

Being slaves to struggle and educating ourselves of illegal hustle bowing to crack cocaine praising vodka and Cîroc all one in the same standing as culprits of blame covered in shame

On pursuit to veil pain, you have forgotten your name

Sr. Jaquan prince Hakeem queen Rashida princess Kesha you are royal

Esteem your mind to the highness of your ancestors

Establish a foot print like your predecessors

Become free from the chains of misery, bonds of catastrophe, and shackles of society

Be introduced to the full plate of proper education eat from it and become full

Taste the juice of knowledge and you will no longer be a fool

Eat ye and drink ye all of it

Still, where are we heading?

Younger generations look up to us and stumble in the path we are treading

And what do they see? Dropout rates that just keep on rising the streets that just keep on swelling there's a wound within the black community that yearns for healing and cries for soothing and as long as we continue to sleep that wound will keep on oozing and become infected like our women who are leading carriers of this deadly epidemic we call aids we need aide

Expelling statistics and stereotype of liking watermelon fried chicken and Kool aid

Or how our black men are seven times more likely to be incarcerated

The power of education shall never become out dated

And the drive for success won't ever be overrated

Be fully persuaded my brothers and sisters
You can either be part of the movement or just an onlooker
Set in your mind that you too can be doctors, lawyers and entrepreneurs
You will then be headed in the right direction
And the royalty within you will experience resurrection
Fulfilling your destination enchanted with education inspired by aspirations
Encouraged by declarations and told to among the nations
You will be great

It Takes A Village

Amir's First Race, 2018

FORD YEARS
2012

The beauty of years graced upon statute merely regarded as ordinary

Extraordinary accounts for such tenderness

To touch one's soul with jewels for eyes and seemingly golden finger tips of passion

Crowned with medallion wisdom, simple utterances like 'child' and 'baby' exceeded terms of endearment, but rather a commitment to passion itself

The beauty of years clothed upon statute that wore classic values, sported morals that even time pondered with honor, suiting her with salute

Hail, mother of elegance for the angels now do style you as heaven's ornament, earth's adornment and Comstock's precious treasure

Life does measure 106 as the ford years; gentle and distinct passing on standards

The beauty of years stored in a woman well-mannered with valor

You lived the beauty of years

In loving memory of Mrs. Catherine Ford who was the City of Winter Park's special treasure and lived 106 beautiful years.

From Jen
B.A.B.Y
2016

What can one say about a woman who meant so much to so many?

What do you call her? For some, friend, confidante, mom, auntie, cousin, grandma

To me, my baby

My B. A. B. Y

B, the BEST and closest friend I'll ever know. Over the span of my entire life, she has nurtured my growth. The BEST listener, the BEST giver, the BEST advisor, one of the BEST people to laugh with and to talk with

A, admirable. I admired her ability to persist and persevere even in moments that didn't seem clear, she always fought hard and stayed strong knowing that God was near

Again B, for bold. Bold enough to withstand life's storms. Bold enough to understand God's master plan. And BOLD enough to be resilient after every tragedy

Y, I ask myself, why'd you have to go so soon

I'll miss you immensely and I'll think about you plenty

My baby, B. The Best. A. The one whose love I admired. B, I have no doubt that I get my boldness from you. And why, I'll try not to ask that, because I know heaven has welcomed you with open And ready arms. For some, friend, confidante, mom, auntie, cousin, grandma

But for me, you were and will always be my baby

In loving memory of her grandmother Rutha L. Hamilton, On behalf of Jenifer Pauldo.

OUR SISTER
2016

There is something about love and the power of its bond

There is something about our sister whose love is so strong

There was something about our sister who was always there, and there was something about the precious and tender ways she would show her care

But what was so awesome and so amazing to see, was how one sister's love was so motherly

One sisters love who had more than enough to stretch, one sisters love who, despite what may always gave her best

Her arms, warm and protecting, her heart pure and reflecting God's spirit

Her voice, soft as a spring breeze, and calming like the buzz of a thousand bees

Our sister, there was something so bold about her, something gold about her

Something so special, speech could not express, pictures could not contest, but those who know her could witness and confess this something special our sister possessed

There's something about love and the power of its bond, there's something about our sister whose love is so strong

So strong and so brave, a love like no other

Our sister's love was like that of a mother

Though absent from the body, never from our hearts

For there was something special about our sister that could never be torn apart

In loving memory of sister Rutha L. Hamilton, on behalf of Luvenia Paige (Rest peacefully), Alice McNeal & Deborah McCain.

Sister-Friend

2020

Intro (from a conversation):

Today, talking with y'all has been like chicken noodle soup for the black woman's soul. It is proof that a strong village of other black women who are committed to the success of their friends, in every way, is like a bridge over troubled waters. Like chili on a cold night, a coat in a wet storm.

Sister-Friend

Girl you walk around here like you got it going on
Chin high, chest higher and strutting like these 99 problems ain't blowing up your phone
I see you over there making everything look easy
But trust me queen I can see through you completely
And yes, I'm calling you out because I can
That's what I'm supposed to do, I'm your sister-friend
I'm calling you to the carpet on your cosmic strength and your brilliant mind
Conquering classrooms, boardrooms, bedrooms and still managing to stay fine
Taking your daily dose of societal nonsense and doing so with such delight
Rising each morning with grit and tenacity ready to take on the days fight
You swing at double standards with a ring on every finger
And you kick the expectations of beauty while maintaining pristine demeanor
Rocking your crown in bold locks, brave braids, and strong fro's
Leaving no room for insecurities, toxicity, negativity or heavy loads
The cost of your oil folks will never know
But from where I stand, it's a divine flow
When your head starts to bow a bit, or when your feet start to feel pain
Know that I'll catch the baton, cancel the plan or just sit with you in the pouring rain
That's what I'm supposed to do I'm your sister friend
Here to nurture your confidence, polish your diamonds, and help you take down your giants
Our sisterhood is not a science
Just a village of powerful women whose bond has formed an alliance

With a love that measures from end to end
You know I got you cause I'm your
Sister-Friend

Dedicated to all of my sister-friends. You know who and whose you are. I love you forever.

MIGHTY GOOD MEN
2015

What a man what a man what a man what a mighty good man
For these men are strong as gusts of wind from a category five hurricane
With ease, he gave land, sea, and animals their irrevocable name
He gave fame to the feminine seed, mother of she, eve
With just one rib, a helpmeet was fulfilled. For these men have strength
For these men are strong and mighty in valor, mighty in courage, mighty in bravery and not by power of muscle alone
These men know the preciousness of their daughters and the value in their sons
And the taste of sacrifice is familiar to their tongue
For these men are more than lawmakers, pastors, fathers, husbands
These men were chosen to be men by a man who said there's a mission to be completed and I think I need a man to do it. For these men are chosen
These men were woven with divine wonder for these men are kings, priest, protectors, providers fighters, riders, igniters
What great men
What a man what a man what a man what mighty good men

In celebration of the 2015 retirees from the City of Winter Park (All departments).

A FAMILY AFFAIR
2010

Sitting together, laughing together, reflecting on memories of things that seem like history

Singing together, praying together, because that's what keeps a family together

Meeting the need of a fellow member who will one day no longer be a borrower, but a lender

The fellowship of loved ones despite long journeys each one have come

We celebrate love and we rise to the occasion of abundance

As we look around we notice a certain vibe that can be found when we are surrounded by family ones that have watched us grow and others we have grown to know

Coming together, sharing together, the elements that help us grow together and create bonds

That will last forever

Smiling at our youngest generation realizing their very simulation when we were that generation. A concentration of the fact that time moves forward not back

And one day that generation will be mothers and fathers of many

Then too will they demonstrate the heart of family which is the art of love

A cherished gift from God above

So, with a room filled with this gift and care, we dedicate this night to a family affair

Mommy, 1978

FIRST LOVE
2013

God trusted you to be the vessel of true, unconditional love
Mommy it's because of you I know what love feels like, sounds like, looks like, smells like
Your signature touch I know because of the countless times you hold me in your arms
Your voice I know as I can hear it clearly above a million sounds
Your face I know because when I look in the mirror, I see your bright smile, your flawless skin, and your beautiful eyes
Your smell I know because it was your fragrance I searched for as a child when I wanted to rest on your chest
Mommy, God knew what was best for me when He made you mine
Thank you for everything, most of all, for teaching me how to love without limits
You will forever be my first love

MOTHER'S DAY
2012

A warm heart with lots of love to give
A healing touch to prove that love lives
A graceful smile and hugs to give away
A soothing voice that comforts dismay
Sweet words that flow from your lips
Makes life a bit easier with every little tip
Signature compassion shown like no other
Makes you special, makes you kind, makes you Mother

M.O.T.H.E.R
2004

Grandma Taught Me Math on Her Hands
2020

Grandma, I need help with my homework
Child don't come in here with all that noise and change out your school shirt
Teacher say I ain't doing so good in math
Go on in there and run you some hot water for a bath
Look at the grade on this last test grandma, I ain't even get a B
Stop all that hollering child and you know good and well I can't see
Well, how I'm supposed to do all this work and I ain't even got no calculator
Girl, you just complaining now, get over here let me feel them papers
Grandma, teacher be talking too fast. I just don't get it
We gon' use fingers and toes until you understand all those digits
First question say five plus foe
Put a 'r' in there girl, don't say that number like that no mo'
I keep messing up the lines when I try to write 'em down
Look up here gal so I ain't gotta keep listening to that frown
One, two, three, four, five, six, seven, eight, nine
Didn't I say you gon' be just fine?
But, grandma I won't have your hands on the test
Before you take it I'll write on yours 'just do your best'
Grandma I might not be so bad in math!
Now let's count how many times I said go take a bath!

All the Love You Can Stand

Philadelphia, 2018

[]

If Ever I Should Love, 1986
1986

If ever I should love
Let me play it by the rules
Whether I be called a saint
Or cast away a fool

Let me learn it to be real
Let me earn it to be true
As it lives a part of me
As I learn the heart of you

If ever I should love
Let it be chaste and warm
Let my life remain a melody
As it plays a cheerful song

Let it grow to the fullest mountain
To its winter snow covered peak
May it play a symphony
May it say the perfect speech

For then if love should fail me
It would go its rightful way
For then no one would need me
And I'll have no game to play

For moments love has been to me
A wonder and a mystery
And sometimes it seems
Of sympathy and a dream

For if in sympathy my heart should yield
The flow of warmth that I may feel
Then let the water from the purest spring
Compose a song for you to sing

If ever I should love
May it be my special creed
To give my best, for only love
could make my heart go free

If ever I should love
May it be of the essence breath
Of a new life clean and fresh

As a jasmine blossom freed
The fragrance of its seed

Then never should I long to be
With the love that call to me
Never will I give
A love that's not for real

If ever I should love
May it be of God and good
That the effort that one man
Gave all the love he could

By: Clarence Jordan
March 11, 1986

Daddy's Poem, March 11, 1986

Clance Jordan at 510 W . Comstock, 1956

If Ever I Should Love, 2019
2019

If ever I should love
Let it fill me up. Let it fill me until running over runs out of room let it move me
Let it move me until stillness has grown jealous, let me relish in this love, if ever I should love
If ever I should love let me know it to be warm let it rain on me in the wildest storm
Let it show me all of its colors and complexions on rainbows and reflections
Let it be gold and let it be good, let me get weathered in this love if ever I should
If ever I should love
If ever I should love let it be wise and let it be well. Let it be Proverbs and the Song of Solomon
Let it be for real. Let me read it without eyes, so that my heart and hands will know the way
Let me feel it in my belly and birth it each day
Let me nurture this love with lips, light, and all things good
If ever I should love, if ever I should
If ever I should love let it know my name. Let it lock its vivid picture in a Victorian frame
The abstract and the concrete tones, let the observers see
All of the beauty in this love that has been painted for me
Let them witness the confident strokes and bold color choices
Let this art of love speak to hearts and voices
Let me know that I know the magnificence of this love
If ever, if ever I should love

Miss You Daddy
11/12/1946 – 07/08/2019

Daddy & I at the Annual MLK Festival
in Hannibal Square Circa 2017

Just finished singing Christmas carols at
510 W. Comstock Circa 2015

CHEVY CRUZ
2016

Drove 1,000 miles with my best pal in a black four door Chevy Cruz with no sun roof
Chance the rapper and the life of Pablo on repeat we awed with glee at the sights of peaks and valleys. By chance, we were having an 'I hope you dance experience'
Embracing mountains in the distance and charging toward the paths of least resistance in a Chevy Cruz that knew no rules
Just used its four wheels to carry two fools who thought they knew love
Sights and songs spoke truths our mouths knew not of while our hearts were keenly aware going 1,000 miles north together, our hearts were going in separate directions at a steady speed
The saving power was at least we weren't going south. Instead, we were going to the extent of which our sins were casted, as far as east is from the west
With the Life of Pablo blasting, we were ignorant to the inevitable crashing of our love
Still we headed north for 1,000 miles in a black four door Chevy Cruz that knew no rules
Just used its four wheels to carry two fools who thought they knew love

All Over Me
2019

I've got this love all over me
Dripping slowly spreading quickly infecting every pulse
With every beat I feel an echo of this love. It's all over me
I indulge in the bite of my lips tasting awakening, savoring flavors
It tastes like full smiles on wide faces
It smells like vanilla and warm hugs that hold on after the touch is gone
It's this love I've got all over me. It feels like a gasp for air and a slow release
A twitch in the knee, a tightening in the belly. A bellow from the deep
I've got this silk all over me drying every bit of dampness. Spreading joy and wiping away defeat this silk that I've got all over
me grips me tightly and there are no more hollow spaces
Soft to touch. Alluring. For special occasion is this silk all over me
I've got this well that runs deep giving water to all who draws from me, never thirsting
Always full and it's all over me. In the deep, in the dark, down there

WHILE YOU WERE SLEEP
2014

I talk about you when you're sleep

I talk about you like a kid talks about his first visit to the zoo, giving every detail of how he felt when the monkey held up his hand to the window, I talk about the potential in your heart

Similar to the way a new mommy holds her newborn

She finds twinkle in his eyes and wide crisp lines that remind her of streams in an Amazon

I could talk marathons about the lines cradled in your neck, I love it, I run my finger down each row then rub across them just to let you know there's security

I talk about you with the emotion of purity touched for the very first time

You penetrate through my thoughts deeply, I'm experiencing love undefined

I talk about how thankful I am for your soul. Thankful for the mold you've outgrown

Thankful for the expressions of love you currently show

I talk about you when you're sleep, like a treasurer talks about his first discovery of gold

I talk about you, the way I dig you in search for answers to all our "why" questions

This expedition has revealed the true mission of why I love you oh so very much, too much at times. Daily I find reasons to talk about you when you're sleep

Soul Food
2017

Can he wait until I get home to make his soul fall right off the bone?
It's Sunday and I want to feed him some really good soul food
Collard greens, mac and cheese and Anita B to set the mood
Soul food so good it sticks the to the rib, heart and mind
Soul food like a pot of neck bones marinated with time
So good it makes you dance a dance and sing a song
And belt melodic moans that cooked on low all night long
Can he wait till I get home to feed him and need him and be with him?
Love making that melts like savory butter atop soft, sweet golden-brown cornbread
Forks scrapping plates as golden-brown eyes roll and roll to the back of the head
Can he wait till I get home so I can make his tender soul slide right off the bone?
I wanna stir up some gravy with sautéed touches and kisses his soul has never known
Can he wait till I get there to serve him on a real glass plate?
And pour his tea from this tree of love with all the refills his soul can take?
I wanna feed him some soul food

I Love You
2018

I love you

Don't let that scare you, push you, pull you, or hold you captive

Let this love I chose for you set you free, the freest free there can be

I love you because I made the choice to. I decided to love you on my knees

I decided to love you when God put you on my mind during meditation

I decided to love you when every time you spoke I was full to overflowing

And still I can never get enough

I love you

My body knows it. I call your name, channel your spirit, and she responds with warm rivers relaxed heartbeats, and a smile that melts away doubt and invites peace

Saying this unlocks a place inside of me that just makes more room for loving you

I love you

Catch these words and hold them

Eat from them when you are hungry, drink from them when you are thirsty

Use them for warmth and air to breathe

May it fill you and comfort you

I love you

In Real Deep
2015

I never thought I'd find love like this
Love like this that would literally make my heart breakout in fits
In fits of passion. In fits of essence cause your love is more than a blessing
Beyond favor. I wake up and wonder how many other ways I can labor
To show my love to this gift I don't deserve. I wish I could put it in the freezer and preserve
The richness of our kisses and the bliss in all of this beautiful and fruitful and fresh love
I stare at you for a reason, not just for a season but year round
I stare at you and your deep, dimensional, sensational, sensual, dark brown eyes
The strides I strive to make to show you how our love is our dream fulfilled into reality
I wanna explore more fantasies and mysteries
Seen and unseen, shallow and deep in your spirit and body
I wanna experience more of you in places I've never witnessed and touch areas that I can replenish with more of our love
I just knew I'd never find a love like this so true and mystical
All good karma and reciprocal cycles of expressions
You're a blessing

BLACK MAN, BLACK MAN

2017

Black man black man have you forgotten the color of the womb that has delivered you?

Black man black man have you grown forgetful to the black on your momma's breast from where you once were fed?

Black man black man why have you abandoned the sacredness of the dark womb, of whom do you aim to please?

Dark knees knelt down and prayed for you. Tears poured down black faces fast for the advancement of your black ass

Black man black man is black no longer worthy to be your wife? Good enough to coat your daughters?

Is it just too damn dark for your own damn good, black man?

Black man black man can I ask you some questions?

What is it that magnifies you to another woman's possession?

What is it that causes you to reject the magic in your own black queens?

What is it that persuades you to ignore the beauty of a black woman's eternal company?

Are we just too damn dark for your own damn good black man?

Black hands rub your belly when you are ailing, black hands hold you closely, tightly, lovingly and connect to your soul when you are wailing, black hands lift you when you are falling, grip you when you are slipping, and black hands touch you in your secret places where only black love has the key

What could it be? Perhaps we are just too damn dark for your own damn good black man

Her dark lips have kissed your pain and tasted your sorrows

Her dark lips have spoken goodwill, good fortune and gold into your today's and tomorrow's

I'm talking to that black man that don't date black women just because he doesn't date black women

Black man don't you know that we love you?

Don't you know there are thrones that await you?

Don't you know that you're my "black brother strong brother there is no one above ya I want you to know that I'm here for you forever true"

And that while you are still a king, know that your crown will never fit quite right without your Black Queen

Black man black man look at yourself. Now look at me and your momma

Our wombs are dark and proud

Our hands black and strong

Our lips are powerful and loud

Our skin black to the bone

Black man black man am I just too damn dark for your own damn good?

IG: art_herjones
artherjones.com

CPSIA information can be obtained
at www.ICGtesting.com
Printed in the USA
BVRC091331130521
607264BV00011B/407

9 781632 218186